ALLEN SMITH

Memorizing Daniel 6 - Daniel and the Lions' Den

Memorize Scripture, Memorize the Bible, and Seal God's Word in Your Heart

First published by Nelaco Press 2021

First edition

ISBN: 978-1-952381-63-8

This book was professionally typeset on Reedsy.
Find out more at reedsy.com

To my Lord and Savior

Contents

Before You Begin

Hey reader, before you begin memorizing scripture, I wanted to say thank you by offering a free gift.

I wrote a book called Memorize the Sermon on the Mount and I'd like to give you a free copy.

Simply text BIBLE to (678) 506-7543 and I'll send you a free copy straight to your inbox.

I've even thrown in a free bonus gift just for you.

I pray it becomes a blessing to you as you seal God's Word in your heart.

Introduction

I would like to start off by saying that I have prayed for you, whoever you are, wherever you are, as you are just beginning to start this journey to memorize a piece of the Bible.

In this book, you're going to memorize Daniel 6.

Daniel 6 tells the very well-known story from the Bible where Daniel, the prophet, is sent to the lions' den by the command of Darius, king of Persia. Daniel had made a name for himself among the other high officials who grew quite jealous of him. They knew full well that Daniel held a very regimented prayer life where he would open the window of the upper chamber of his home which pointed toward Jerusalem and prays to God. This he did three times a day.

The other high officials decided to trick Darius into issuing a decree, one that Darius himself couldn't revoke, that no one for 30 days could pray to any god or man but to Darius himself. Anyone who violates the decree would be sent to the lions' den. Daniel, knowing full well the decree had been signed, prayed that same day giving thanks to God as he always had and was reported to Darius by the high officials. As a result, he was thrown in with the lions and, well, you know the rest of the story.

At 28 verses, it will take some work on your part to commit the passage to memory.

This is a game of repetition over time and this book will guide you every step of the way.

That said, there are no tricks, magic strategies, or brain hacks to make it work.

It just takes work but work that is incredibly rewarding.

But even with all that said, there are probably excuses piling up in your head.

Little lies telling you a thousand reasons why you can't possibly remember a section of the Bible.

"I have a bad memory."

"I don't have enough time."

And many other reasons why you might tell yourself this won't work.

Memorizing a passage of the Bible can feel daunting but you don't need to start off by memorizing everything at once.

You just need to start with one verse.

And with that, you're ready to head to the next chapter to learn how to use this book.

How To Use This Book

By now you are probably curious how this book will work so I will quickly give you an overview.

This book covers the entire chapter of Daniel 6, English Standard Version.

This passage of scripture is broken down verse by verse and I recommend you memorize one verse each day working your way through memorizing the entire passage.

Each verse has one dedicated chapter and as mentioned before, this book uses the ESV (English Standard Version) translation. You will be guided to either repeat or recite a verse or verses during each chapter.

This book is set up so that you don't need to have your Bible in front of you to read from.

There are a handful of chapters, though optional, that are the weekly preparation chapters involving some optional prep work. This prep work will make memorizing the entire passage significantly easier and time well spent on your journey to memorizing God's Word. I highly recommend you do it, but feel free to skip it.

Also, I do not require you to say the verse number when memorizing scripture.

The original scriptures were not numbered into verses so I don't believe that is a critical piece to remember. However, if you would like to state the verse number when reciting each verse, you are more than welcome to.

As you work your way through memorizing each verse, there will be days where you will get frustrated. It will seem the verse just won't stick. That is completely normal. Some verses will be significantly harder to memorize than others. That is okay. Don't be afraid to repeat a chapter if you feel you didn't quite memorize the verse that day.

If the first round of repetition didn't help it stick, the second or third round should surely do the trick.

You are ready to begin on a wonderful, spirit-filled journey to solidify a piece of God's Word inside of your heart.

May it be an incredible blessing on your life and your personal walk with Christ.

Week 1 Prep Work

Welcome to the preparation work on your journey to memorizing Daniel 6.

Like I mentioned in the introduction, this work is completely optional, but I cannot encourage you enough to do the prep work.

If you had four hours to chop down a tree with a dull axe, you would be better off sharpening your axe for two of those four hours before getting started.

This prep work is sharpening your axe.

It will make everything moving forward significantly easier.

Though it will take time, this will be time well spent which you may not realize until you begin memorizing each verse one by one.

To complete the prep work, you will need to read the passage out loud 50 times.

Sounds daunting, doesn't it?

Reading out loud Daniel 6 would take roughly 7 minutes. Do that 50 times and you are looking at roughly 6 hours worth of reading out loud.

Not many people would have the luxury in spare time to squeeze that in and

I'm not asking you to.

Instead of doing the entire passage in one go, you are going to do a smaller chunk that would allow you to accomplish the task in an hour or less.

You are going to focus on just the first six verses as you read them out loud 50 times.

Don't have an hour?

Do it for 30 minutes running through them 25 times.

Or commit to what you can. I assure you, whatever you do here will help.

Whenever you try to memorize something from scratch, it can feel like there is a lot of resistance to get the material to stick in your brain.

But if you are very familiar with whatever you are trying to commit to memory, it is like globbing memory glue on it before you get started.

After each week, you will have an opportunity to attempt the next block of 6 verses for the following week.

If you have decided to do the prep work, get ready to read the following chunk of verses out loud. Oh, and grab a glass of water. Your mouth can get pretty dry doing this prep work.

Please note, I left the verse numbers in the passage on the following page for your reference only.

When you are ready, begin.

1 It pleased Darius to set over the kingdom 120 satraps, to be throughout the whole kingdom; 2 and over them three high officials, of whom Daniel was one, to whom these satraps should give account, so that the king might suffer no loss. 3 Then this Daniel became distinguished above all the other high officials and satraps, because an excellent spirit was in him. And the king planned to set him over the whole kingdom. 4 Then the high officials and the satraps sought to find a ground for complaint against Daniel with regard to the kingdom, but they could find no ground for complaint or any fault, because he was faithful, and no error or fault was found in him. 5 Then these men said, "We shall not find any ground for complaint against this Daniel unless we find it in connection with the law of his God." 6 Then these high officials and satraps came by agreement to the king and said to him, "O King Darius, live forever!" (Daniel 6:1-6 ESV)

See you tomorrow!

Daniel 6:1

Today you are going to memorize Daniel 6:1.

You are going to memorize the verse by using the 10-10-10 method.

To use this method, each verse will be repeated out loud 10 times and then immediately recited 10 times from memory. In later chapters, you'll start combining verses and reciting those 10 times as well.

Don't worry if that was a little confusing to follow. Just follow the instructions and you will do just fine.

I understand 10 times may seem excessive and tedious, but trust me, this is necessary. There will be times where it may take you speaking a verse 5 times or more just to fully nail it down before being able to recite it from memory.

As a last word of advice before you begin, I wanted to share with you a few tips that have helped me memorize scripture:

1. Speaking the verse with conviction or emotion as you repeat or recite it from memory.
2. Emphasizing a different word each time you say it out loud.
3. Use hand motions as you speak.
4. Creating images in your head corresponding to each piece of a verse.

5. Singing a verse or a piece of a verse instead of speaking it.

Yes, you heard that last one right. It's weird, it works, but don't feel you need to incorporate all of these at once or any at all. As you go deeper into memorizing scripture, you will find what works for you and what doesn't.

Let's begin.

Say the following verse out loud ten times. You do not have to say the citation within the parenthesis.

"It pleased Darius to set over the kingdom 120 satraps, to be throughout the whole kingdom" (Daniel 6:1).

When you are done, recite the verse ten times in a row from memory, doing your best not to look at the verse.

Great job! You got your first verse down!

Throughout your day when you are driving your car, taking a break from work, or cooking a meal, go over what you've memorized so far to keep reinforcing it in your mind.

Tomorrow you'll quickly review what you learned today and add another verse to it.

If you don't feel confident you've truly memorized today's verse, consider going through the chapter again.

See you tomorrow!

God Bless.

Daniel 6:2

Today you are going to memorize Daniel 6:2.

After you review what you have already learned, you are going to memorize today's verse using the 10-10-10 Method.

Let's begin.

Let's review the verse you learned yesterday by reciting it 10 times from memory. Glance over it if you need a refresher.

"It pleased Darius to set over the kingdom 120 satraps, to be throughout the whole kingdom" (Daniel 6:1).

When your review is done, let's get into today's verse.

Say the following verse out loud 10 times.

"And over them three high officials, of whom Daniel was one, to whom these satraps should give account, so that the king might suffer no loss" (Daniel 6:2).

When you are done, recite the verse 10 times in a row from memory, doing your best not to look at the verse.

Great job! You got your next verse down!

You know the drill. Throughout your day when you're driving to work, taking a break from work, or cooking a meal, go over what you've memorized so far to keep reinforcing it in your mind.

Tomorrow you'll quickly review what you learned today and add another verse to it.

If you don't feel confident you've truly memorized today's verse, consider listening through the chapter again.

See you tomorrow!

Good Bless

Daniel 6:3

Today you are going to memorize Daniel 6:3.

After you review what you have already learned, you are going to memorize today's verse using the 10-10-10 Method.

Let's begin.

Let's review the verse you learned yesterday by reciting it 10 times from memory. Glance over it if you need a refresher.

"And over them three high officials, of whom Daniel was one, to whom these satraps should give account, so that the king might suffer no loss" (Daniel 6:2).

Now you're going to review all the verses you have memorized up to this point by reciting them 10 times. You can find it in the prep work chapter for this week if you need a refresher. If after three times you feel confident in your ability to recite all the verses you have currently memorized, feel free to call it good enough.

When your review is done, let's get into today's verse.

Say the following verse out loud 10 times:

"Then this Daniel became distinguished above all the other high officials and satraps, because an excellent spirit was in him. And the king planned to set him over the whole kingdom" (Daniel 6:3).

When you are done, recite the verse 10 times in a row from memory, doing your best not to look at the verse.

Great job! You got your next verse down!

You know the drill, throughout your day when you're driving to work, taking a break from work, or cooking a meal, go over what you've memorized so far to keep reinforcing it in your mind.

Tomorrow you'll quickly review what you learned today and add another verse to it.

If you don't feel confident you've truly memorized today's verse, consider listening through the chapter again.

See you tomorrow!

God bless.

Daniel 6:4

Today you are going to memorize Daniel 6:4.

After you review what you have already learned, you are going to memorize today's verse using the 10-10-10 Method.

Let's begin.

Let's review the verse you learned yesterday by reciting it 10 times from memory. Glance over it if you need a refresher.

"Then this Daniel became distinguished above all the other high officials and satraps, because an excellent spirit was in him. And the king planned to set him over the whole kingdom" (Daniel 6:3).

Now you're going to review all the verses you have memorized up to this point by reciting them 10 times. You can find it in the prep work chapter for this week if you need a refresher. If after three times you feel confident in your ability to recite all the verses you have currently memorized, feel free to call it good enough.

When your review is done, let's get into today's verse.

Say the following verse out loud 10 times:

"Then the high officials and the satraps sought to find a ground for complaint against Daniel with regard to the kingdom, but they could find no ground for complaint or any fault, because he was faithful, and no error or fault was found in him" (Daniel 6:4).

When you are done, recite the verse 10 times in a row from memory, doing your best not to look at the verse.

Great job! You got your next verse down!

You know the drill, throughout your day when you're driving to work, taking a break from work, or cooking a meal, go over what you've memorized so far to keep reinforcing it in your mind.

Tomorrow you'll quickly review what you learned today and add another verse to it.

If you don't feel confident you've truly memorized today's verse, consider listening through the chapter again.

See you tomorrow!

God bless.

Daniel 6:5

Today you are going to memorize Daniel 6:5.

After you review what you have already learned, you are going to memorize today's verse using the 10-10-10 Method.

Let's begin.

Let's review the verse you learned yesterday by reciting it 10 times from memory. Glance over it if you need a refresher.

"Then the high officials and the satraps sought to find a ground for complaint against Daniel with regard to the kingdom, but they could find no ground for complaint or any fault, because he was faithful, and no error or fault was found in him" (Daniel 6:4).

Now you're going to review all the verses you have memorized up to this point by reciting them 10 times. You can find it in the prep work chapter for this week if you need a refresher. If after three times you feel confident in your ability to recite all the verses you have currently memorized, feel free to call it good enough.

When your review is done, let's get into today's verse.

Say the following verse out loud 10 times:

"Then these men said, 'We shall not find any ground for complaint against this Daniel unless we find it in connection with the law of his God'" (Daniel 6:5).

When you are done, recite the verse 10 times in a row from memory, doing your best not to look at the verse.

Great job! You got your next verse down!

You know the drill, throughout your day when you're driving to work, taking a break from work, or cooking a meal, go over what you've memorized so far to keep reinforcing it in your mind.

Tomorrow you'll quickly review what you learned today and add another verse to it.

If you don't feel confident you've truly memorized today's verse, consider listening through the chapter again.

See you tomorrow!

God bless.

Daniel 6:6

Today you are going to memorize Daniel 6:6.

After you review what you have already learned, you are going to memorize today's verse using the 10-10-10 Method.

Let's begin.

Let's review the verse you learned yesterday by reciting it 10 times from memory. Glance over it if you need a refresher.

"Then these men said, 'We shall not find any ground for complaint against this Daniel unless we find it in connection with the law of his God'" (Daniel 6:5).

Now you're going to review all the verses you have memorized up to this point by reciting them 10 times. You can find it in the prep work chapter for this week if you need a refresher. If after three times you feel confident in your ability to recite all the verses you have currently memorized, feel free to call it good enough.

When your review is done, let's get into today's verse.

Say the following verse out loud 10 times:

"Then these high officials and satraps came by agreement to the king and said to him, 'O King Darius, live forever!'" (Daniel 6:6).

When you are done, recite the verse 10 times in a row from memory, doing your best not to look at the verse.

Great job! You got your next verse down and your first block of 6 verses, too!

With your first block of verses completed, I would love to hear what you think so far about the book in the form of a review.

Reviews help other listeners find this book so that they too can become more intimate with God's Word.

Better yet, leaving a review is easy.

Simply go to the book's page on Amazon, scroll down and click the 'leave a customer review' button, choose a rating, leave a few words, and you're done!

Bonus points for leaving a picture with your review.

Super bonus points for a video.

Just a few minutes of your time will help people from all over the world, people you may never meet in this life, find this book and seal God's Word in their hearts.

Tomorrow you have the optional prep work for the next block of 6 verses. Though it's not mandatory, I can't stress enough how beneficial it will be moving forward.

If you plan to skip it, simply move to the following chapter to begin memorizing the first verse of the next block of 6 verses.

See you tomorrow!

God Bless!

Week 2 Prep Work

If you are here, that tells me you are ready for your next block of verses to memorize.

Great job so far. I know it takes a lot of time and effort to memorize scripture and I hope all that time and effort has been a joyful experience.

Just like with the first round of prep work, this is completely optional.

You are not required to do this to memorize the last block of 7 verses.

But like I said before, it will make the task much easier.

If you are not up for the prep work, feel free to skip this chapter.

If you are willing to give it a shot, get ready to read the next 7 verses out loud 50 times which will take you about an hour.

If you don't have an hour, run through them 25 times which will only take you about 30 minutes.

Or commit to whatever you can.

Anything and everything you do here will help moving forward.

Please note, I left the verse numbers in the passage for your reference only.

When you are ready, begin.

7 All the high officials of the kingdom, the prefects and the satraps, the
counselors and the governors are agreed that the king should establish an
ordinance and enforce an injunction, that whoever makes petition to any god
or man for thirty days, except to you, O king, shall be cast into the den of
lions. 8 Now, O king, establish the injunction and sign the document, so that
it cannot be changed, according to the law of the Medes and the Persians,
which cannot be revoked." 9 Therefore King Darius signed the document
and injunction. 10 When Daniel knew that the document had been signed, he
went to his house where he had windows in his upper chamber open toward
Jerusalem. He got down on his knees three times a day and prayed and gave
thanks before his God, as he had done previously. 11 Then these men came by
agreement and found Daniel making petition and plea before his God. 12 Then
they came near and said before the king, concerning the injunction, "O king!
Did you not sign an injunction, that anyone who makes petition to any god
or man within thirty days except to you, O king, shall be cast into the den of
lions?" The king answered and said, "The thing stands fast, according to the
law of the Medes and Persians, which cannot be revoked." (Daniel 6:7-12)

See you tomorrow!

Phonetic Pronunciation:

Medes: meeds

Daniel 6:7

Today you are going to memorize Daniel 6:7.

After you review what you have already learned, you are going to memorize today's verse using the 10-10-10 Method.

Let's begin.

Let's review the verse you learned last by reciting it 10 times from memory. Glance over it if you need a refresher.

"Then these high officials and satraps came by agreement to the king and said to him, 'O King Darius, live forever!'" (Daniel 6:6).

Now you're going to review all the verses you have memorized up to this point by reciting them 10 times. You can find it in the prep work chapter for this week if you need a refresher. If after three times you feel confident in your ability to recite all the verses you have currently memorized, feel free to call it good enough.

When your review is done, let's get into today's verse.

Say the following verse out loud 10 times:

"'All the high officials of the kingdom, the prefects and the satraps, the counselors and the governors are agreed that the king should establish an ordinance and enforce an injunction, that whoever makes petition to any god or man for thirty days, except to you, O king, shall be cast into the den of lions'" (Daniel 6:7).

When you are done, recite the verse 10 times in a row from memory, doing your best not to look at the verse.

Great job! You got your next verse down!

You know the drill, throughout your day when you're driving to work, taking a break from work, or cooking a meal, go over what you've memorized so far to keep reinforcing it in your mind.

Tomorrow you'll quickly review what you learned today and add another verse to it.

If you don't feel confident you've truly memorized today's verse, consider listening through the chapter again.

See you tomorrow!

God bless.

Daniel 6:8

Today you are going to memorize Daniel 6:8.

After you review what you have already learned, you are going to memorize today's verse using the 10-10-10 Method.

Let's begin.

Let's review the verse you learned yesterday by reciting it 10 times from memory. Glance over it if you need a refresher.

"'All the high officials of the kingdom, the prefects and the satraps, the counselors and the governors are agreed that the king should establish an ordinance and enforce an injunction, that whoever makes petition to any god or man for thirty days, except to you, O king, shall be cast into the den of lions'" (Daniel 6:7).

Now you're going to review all the verses you have memorized up to this point by reciting them 10 times. You can find it in the prep work chapter for this week if you need a refresher. If after three times you feel confident in your ability to recite all the verses you have currently memorized, feel free to call it good enough.

When your review is done, let's get into today's verse.

Say the following verse out loud 10 times:

"'Now, O king, establish the injunction and sign the document, so that it cannot be changed, according to the law of the Medes and the Persians, which cannot be revoked'" (Daniel 6:8).

When you are done, recite the verse 10 times in a row from memory, doing your best not to look at the verse.

Great job! You got your next verse down!

You know the drill, throughout your day when you're driving to work, taking a break from work, or cooking a meal, go over what you've memorized so far to keep reinforcing it in your mind.

Tomorrow you'll quickly review what you learned today and add another verse to it.

If you don't feel confident you've truly memorized today's verse, consider listening through the chapter again.

See you tomorrow!

God bless.

Daniel 6:9

Today you are going to memorize Daniel 6:9.

After you review what you have already learned, you are going to memorize today's verse using the 10-10-10 Method.

Let's begin.

Let's review the verse you learned yesterday by reciting it 10 times from memory. Glance over it if you need a refresher.

"'Now, O king, establish the injunction and sign the document, so that it cannot be changed, according to the law of the Medes and the Persians, which cannot be revoked'" (Daniel 6:8).

Now you're going to review all the verses you have memorized up to this point by reciting them 10 times. You can find it in the prep work chapter for this week if you need a refresher. If after three times you feel confident in your ability to recite all the verses you have currently memorized, feel free to call it good enough.

When your review is done, let's get into today's verse.

Say the following verse out loud 10 times:

"Therefore King Darius signed the document and injunction" (Daniel 6:9).

When you are done, recite the verse 10 times in a row from memory, doing your best not to look at the verse.

Great job! You got your next verse down!

You know the drill, throughout your day when you're driving to work, taking a break from work, or cooking a meal, go over what you've memorized so far to keep reinforcing it in your mind.

Tomorrow you'll quickly review what you learned today and add another verse to it.

If you don't feel confident you've truly memorized today's verse, consider listening through the chapter again.

See you tomorrow!

God bless.

Daniel 6:10

Today you are going to memorize Daniel 6:10.

After you review what you have already learned, you are going to memorize today's verse using the 10-10-10 Method.

Let's begin.

Let's review the verse you learned yesterday by reciting it 10 times from memory. Glance over it if you need a refresher.

"Therefore King Darius signed the document and injunction" (Daniel 6:9).

Now you're going to review all the verses you have memorized up to this point by reciting them 10 times. You can find it in the prep work chapter for this week if you need a refresher. If after three times you feel confident in your ability to recite all the verses you have currently memorized, feel free to call it good enough.

When your review is done, let's get into today's verse.

Say the following verse out loud 10 times:

"When Daniel knew that the document had been signed, he went to his

house where he had windows in his upper chamber open toward Jerusalem. He got down on his knees three times a day and prayed and gave thanks before his God, as he had done previously" (Daniel 6:10).

When you are done, recite the verse 10 times in a row from memory, doing your best not to look at the verse.

Great job! You got your next verse down!

You know the drill, throughout your day when you're driving to work, taking a break from work, or cooking a meal, go over what you've memorized so far to keep reinforcing it in your mind.

Tomorrow you'll quickly review what you learned today and add another verse to it.

If you don't feel confident you've truly memorized today's verse, consider listening through the chapter again.

See you tomorrow!

God bless.

Daniel 6:11

Today you are going to memorize Daniel 6:11.

After you review what you have already learned, you are going to memorize today's verse using the 10-10-10 Method.

Let's begin.

Let's review the verse you learned yesterday by reciting it 10 times from memory. Glance over it if you need a refresher.

"When Daniel knew that the document had been signed, he went to his house where he had windows in his upper chamber open toward Jerusalem. He got down on his knees three times a day and prayed and gave thanks before his God, as he had done previously" (Daniel 6:10).

Now you're going to review all the verses you have memorized up to this point by reciting them 10 times. You can find it in the prep work chapter for this week if you need a refresher. If after three times you feel confident in your ability to recite all the verses you have currently memorized, feel free to call it good enough.

When your review is done, let's get into today's verse.

Say the following verse out loud 10 times:

"Then these men came by agreement and found Daniel making petition and plea before his God" (Daniel 6:11).

When you are done, recite the verse 10 times in a row from memory, doing your best not to look at the verse.

Great job! You got your next verse down!

You know the drill, throughout your day when you're driving to work, taking a break from work, or cooking a meal, go over what you've memorized so far to keep reinforcing it in your mind.

Tomorrow you'll quickly review what you learned today and add another verse to it.

If you don't feel confident you've truly memorized today's verse, consider listening through the chapter again.

See you tomorrow!

God bless.

Daniel 6:12

Today you are going to memorize Daniel 6:12.

After you review what you have already learned, you are going to memorize today's verse using the 10-10-10 Method.

Let's begin.

Let's review the verse you learned yesterday by reciting it 10 times from memory. Glance over it if you need a refresher.

"Then these men came by agreement and found Daniel making petition and plea before his God" (Daniel 6:11).

Now you're going to review all the verses you have memorized up to this point by reciting them 10 times. You can find it in the prep work chapter for this week if you need a refresher. If after three times you feel confident in your ability to recite all the verses you have currently memorized, feel free to call it good enough.

When your review is done, let's get into today's verse.

Say the following verse out loud 10 times:

"Then they came near and said before the king, concerning the injunction, 'O king! Did you not sign an injunction, that anyone who makes petition to any god or man within thirty days except to you, O king, shall be cast into the den of lions?' The king answered and said, 'The thing stands fast, according to the law of the Medes and Persians, which cannot be revoked'" (Daniel 6:12).

When you are done, recite the verse 10 times in a row from memory, doing your best not to look at the verse.

Great job! You got your next verse down!

You know the drill, throughout your day when you're driving to work, taking a break from work, or cooking a meal, go over what you've memorized so far to keep reinforcing it in your mind.

Tomorrow you have the optional prep work for the next block of 6 verses. Though it's not mandatory, I can't stress enough how beneficial it will be moving forward.

If you plan to skip it, simply move to the following chapter to begin memorizing the first verse of the next block of 6 verses.

If you don't feel confident you've truly memorized today's verse, consider listening through the chapter again.

See you tomorrow!

God bless.

Week 3 Prep Work

If you are here, that tells me you are ready for your next block of verses to memorize.

Great job so far. I know it takes a lot of time and effort to memorize scripture and I hope all that time and effort has been a joyful experience.

Just like with the first round of prep work, this is completely optional.

You are not required to do this to memorize the last block of 7 verses.

But like I said before, it will make the task much easier.

If you are not up for the prep work, feel free to skip this chapter.

If you are willing to give it a shot, get ready to read the next 7 verses out loud 50 times which will take you about an hour.

If you don't have an hour, run through them 25 times which will only take you about 30 minutes.

Or commit to whatever you can.

Anything and everything you do here will help moving forward.

Please note, I left the verse numbers in the passage for your reference only.

When you are ready, begin.

13 Then they answered and said before the king, "Daniel, who is one of the exiles from Judah, pays no attention to you, O king, or the injunction you have signed, but makes his petition three times a day." 14 Then the king, when he heard these words, was much distressed and set his mind to deliver Daniel. And he labored till the sun went down to rescue him. 15 Then these men came by agreement to the king and said to the king, "Know, O king, that it is a law of the Medes and Persians that no injunction or ordinance that the king establishes can be changed." 16 Then the king commanded, and Daniel was brought and cast into the den of lions. The king declared to Daniel, "May your God, whom you serve continually, deliver you!" 17 And a stone was brought and laid on the mouth of the den, and the king sealed it with his own signet and with the signet of his lords, that nothing might be changed concerning Daniel. 18 Then the king went to his palace and spent the night fasting; no diversions were brought to him, and sleep fled from him. (Daniel 6:13-18)

See you tomorrow!

Phonetic Pronunciation:
Medes: meeds

Daniel 6:13

Today you are going to memorize Daniel 6:13.

After you review what you have already learned, you are going to memorize today's verse using the 10-10-10 Method.

Let's begin.

Let's review the verse you learned yesterday by reciting it 10 times from memory. Glance over it if you need a refresher.

"Then they came near and said before the king, concerning the injunction, 'O king! Did you not sign an injunction, that anyone who makes petition to any god or man within thirty days except to you, O king, shall be cast into the den of lions?' The king answered and said, 'The thing stands fast, according to the law of the Medes and Persians, which cannot be revoked'" (Daniel 6:12).

Now you're going to review all the verses you have memorized up to this point by reciting them 10 times. You can find it in the prep work chapter for this week if you need a refresher. If after three times you feel confident in your ability to recite all the verses you have currently memorized, feel free to call it good enough.

When your review is done, let's get into today's verse.

Say the following verse out loud 10 times:

"Then they answered and said before the king, 'Daniel, who is one of the exiles from Judah, pays no attention to you, O king, or the injunction you have signed, but makes his petition three times a day'" (Daniel 6:13).

When you are done, recite the verse 10 times in a row from memory, doing your best not to look at the verse.

Great job! You got your last verse down!

You know the drill, throughout your day when you are driving your car, taking a break from work, or cooking a meal, go over what you have memorized so far to keep reinforcing it in your mind.

If by chance you don't feel confident you have truly memorized today's verse, consider listening through the chapter again.

God Bless!

Daniel 6:14

Today you are going to memorize Daniel 6:14.

After you review what you have already learned, you are going to memorize today's verse using the 10-10-10 Method.

Let's begin.

Let's review the verse you learned last by reciting it 10 times from memory. Glance over it if you need a refresher.

"Then they answered and said before the king, 'Daniel, who is one of the exiles from Judah, pays no attention to you, O king, or the injunction you have signed, but makes his petition three times a day'" (Daniel 6:13).

Now you're going to review all the verses you have memorized up to this point by reciting them 10 times. You can find it in the prep work chapter for this week if you need a refresher. If after three times you feel confident in your ability to recite all the verses you have currently memorized, feel free to call it good enough.

When your review is done, let's get into today's verse.

Say the following verse out loud 10 times:

"Then the king, when he heard these words, was much distressed and set his mind to deliver Daniel. And he labored till the sun went down to rescue him" (Daniel 6:14).

When you are done, recite the verse 10 times in a row from memory, doing your best not to look at the verse.

Great job! You got your next verse down!

You know the drill, throughout your day when you're driving to work, taking a break from work, or cooking a meal, go over what you've memorized so far to keep reinforcing it in your mind.

Tomorrow you'll quickly review what you learned today and add another verse to it.

If you don't feel confident you've truly memorized today's verse, consider listening through the chapter again.

See you tomorrow!

God bless.

Daniel 6:15

Today you are going to memorize Daniel 6:15.

After you review what you have already learned, you are going to memorize today's verse using the 10-10-10 Method.

Let's begin.

Let's review the verse you learned yesterday by reciting it 10 times from memory. Glance over it if you need a refresher.

"Then the king, when he heard these words, was much distressed and set his mind to deliver Daniel. And he labored till the sun went down to rescue him" (Daniel 6:14).

Now you're going to review all the verses you have memorized up to this point by reciting them 10 times. You can find it in the prep work chapter for this week if you need a refresher. If after three times you feel confident in your ability to recite all the verses you have currently memorized, feel free to call it good enough.

When your review is done, let's get into today's verse.

Say the following verse out loud 10 times:

"Then these men came by agreement to the king and said to the king, 'Know, O king, that it is a law of the Medes and Persians that no injunction or ordinance that the king establishes can be changed'" (Daniel 6:15).

When you are done, recite the verse 10 times in a row from memory, doing your best not to look at the verse.

Great job! You got your next verse down!

You know the drill, throughout your day when you're driving to work, taking a break from work, or cooking a meal, go over what you've memorized so far to keep reinforcing it in your mind.

Tomorrow you'll quickly review what you learned today and add another verse to it.

If you don't feel confident you've truly memorized today's verse, consider listening through the chapter again.

See you tomorrow!

God bless.

Daniel 6:16

Today you are going to memorize Daniel 6:16.

After you review what you have already learned, you are going to memorize today's verse using the 10-10-10 Method.

Let's begin.

Let's review the verse you learned yesterday by reciting it 10 times from memory. Glance over it if you need a refresher.

"Then these men came by agreement to the king and said to the king, 'Know, O king, that it is a law of the Medes and Persians that no injunction or ordinance that the king establishes can be changed;" (Daniel 6:15).

Now you're going to review all the verses you have memorized up to this point by reciting them 10 times. You can find it in the prep work chapter for this week if you need a refresher. If after three times you feel confident in your ability to recite all the verses you have currently memorized, feel free to call it good enough.

When your review is done, let's get into today's verse.

Say the following verse out loud 10 times:

"Then the king commanded, and Daniel was brought and cast into the den of lions. The king declared to Daniel, 'May your God, whom you serve continually, deliver you!;" (Daniel 6:16).

When you are done, recite the verse 10 times in a row from memory, doing your best not to look at the verse.

Great job! You got your next verse down!

You know the drill, throughout your day when you're driving to work, taking a break from work, or cooking a meal, go over what you've memorized so far to keep reinforcing it in your mind.

Tomorrow you'll quickly review what you learned today and add another verse to it.

If you don't feel confident you've truly memorized today's verse, consider listening through the chapter again.

See you tomorrow!

God bless.

Daniel 6:17

Today you are going to memorize Daniel 6:17.

After you review what you have already learned, you are going to memorize today's verse using the 10-10-10 Method.

Let's begin.

Let's review the verse you learned yesterday by reciting it 10 times from memory. Glance over it if you need a refresher.

"Then the king commanded, and Daniel was brought and cast into the den of lions. The king declared to Daniel, 'May your God, whom you serve continually, deliver you!;" (Daniel 6:16).

Now you're going to review all the verses you have memorized up to this point by reciting them 10 times. You can find it in the prep work chapter for this week if you need a refresher. If after three times you feel confident in your ability to recite all the verses you have currently memorized, feel free to call it good enough.

When your review is done, let's get into today's verse.

Say the following verse out loud 10 times:

"And a stone was brought and laid on the mouth of the den, and the king sealed it with his own signet and with the signet of his lords, that nothing might be changed concerning Daniel" (Daniel 6:17).

When you are done, recite the verse 10 times in a row from memory, doing your best not to look at the verse.

Great job! You got your next verse down!

You know the drill, throughout your day when you're driving to work, taking a break from work, or cooking a meal, go over what you've memorized so far to keep reinforcing it in your mind.

Tomorrow you'll quickly review what you learned today and add another verse to it.

If you don't feel confident you've truly memorized today's verse, consider listening through the chapter again.

See you tomorrow!

God bless.

Daniel 6:18

Today you are going to memorize Daniel 6:18.

After you review what you have already learned, you are going to memorize today's verse using the 10-10-10 Method.

Let's begin.

Let's review the verse you learned yesterday by reciting it 10 times from memory. Glance over it if you need a refresher.

"And a stone was brought and laid on the mouth of the den, and the king sealed it with his own signet and with the signet of his lords, that nothing might be changed concerning Daniel" (Daniel 6:17).

Now you're going to review all the verses you have memorized up to this point by reciting them 10 times. You can find it in the prep work chapter for this week if you need a refresher. If after three times you feel confident in your ability to recite all the verses you have currently memorized, feel free to call it good enough.

When your review is done, let's get into today's verse.

Say the following verse out loud 10 times:

"Then the king went to his palace and spent the night fasting; no diversions were brought to him, and sleep fled from him" (Daniel 6:18).

When you are done, recite the verse 10 times in a row from memory, doing your best not to look at the verse.

Great job! You got your next verse down!

You know the drill, throughout your day when you're driving to work, taking a break from work, or cooking a meal, go over what you've memorized so far to keep reinforcing it in your mind.

Tomorrow you have the optional prep work for the next block of 6 verses. Though it's not mandatory, I can't stress enough how beneficial it will be moving forward.

If you plan to skip it, simply move to the following chapter to begin memorizing the first verse of the next block of 6 verses.

If you don't feel confident you've truly memorized today's verse, consider listening through the chapter again.

See you tomorrow!

God bless.

Week 4 Prep Work

If you are here, that tells me you are ready for your next block of verses to memorize.

Great job so far. I know it takes a lot of time and effort to memorize scripture and I hope all that time and effort has been a joyful experience.

Just like with the first round of prep work, this is completely optional.

You are not required to do this to memorize the last block of 7 verses.

But like I said before, it will make the task much easier.

If you are not up for the prep work, feel free to skip this chapter.

If you are willing to give it a shot, get ready to read the next 7 verses out loud 50 times which will take you about an hour.

If you don't have an hour, run through them 25 times which will only take you about 30 minutes.

Or commit to whatever you can.

Anything and everything you do here will help moving forward.

Please note, I left the verse numbers in the passage for your reference only.

When you are ready, begin.

19 Then, at break of day, the king arose and went in haste to the den of lions. 20
As he came near to the den where Daniel was, he cried out in a tone of anguish.
The king declared to Daniel, "O Daniel, servant of the living God, has your God,
whom you serve continually, been able to deliver you from the lions?" 21 Then
Daniel said to the king, "O king, live forever! 22 My God sent his angel and
shut the lions' mouths, and they have not harmed me, because I was found
blameless before him; and also before you, O king, I have done no harm." 23
Then the king was exceedingly glad, and commanded that Daniel be taken up
out of the den. So Daniel was taken up out of the den, and no kind of harm was
found on him, because he had trusted in his God. 24 And the king commanded,
and those men who had maliciously accused Daniel were brought and cast
into the den of lions—they, their children, and their wives. And before they
reached the bottom of the den, the lions overpowered them and broke all their
bones in pieces. (Daniel 6:19-24)

See you tomorrow!

Daniel 6:19

Today you are going to memorize Daniel 6:19.

After you review what you have already learned, you are going to memorize today's verse using the 10-10-10 Method.

Let's begin.

Let's review the verse you learned yesterday by reciting it 10 times from memory. Glance over it if you need a refresher.

"Then the king went to his palace and spent the night fasting; no diversions were brought to him, and sleep fled from him" (Daniel 6:18).

Now you're going to review all the verses you have memorized up to this point by reciting them 10 times. You can find it in the prep work chapter for this week if you need a refresher. If after three times you feel confident in your ability to recite all the verses you have currently memorized, feel free to call it good enough.

When your review is done, let's get into today's verse.

Say the following verse out loud 10 times:

"Then, at break of day, the king arose and went in haste to the den of lions" (Daniel 6:19).

When you are done, recite the verse 10 times in a row from memory, doing your best not to look at the verse.

Great job! You got your next verse down!

You know the drill, throughout your day when you're driving to work, taking a break from work, or cooking a meal, go over what you've memorized so far to keep reinforcing it in your mind.

Tomorrow you'll quickly review what you learned today and add another verse to it.

If you don't feel confident you've truly memorized today's verse, consider listening through the chapter again.

See you tomorrow!

God bless.

Daniel 6:20

Today you are going to memorize Daniel 6:20.

After you review what you have already learned, you are going to memorize today's verse using the 10-10-10 Method.

Let's begin.

Let's review the verse you learned last by reciting it 10 times from memory. Glance over it if you need a refresher.

"Then, at break of day, the king arose and went in haste to the den of lions" (Daniel 6:19).

Now you're going to review all the verses you have memorized up to this point by reciting them 10 times. You can find it in the prep work chapter for this week if you need a refresher. If after three times you feel confident in your ability to recite all the verses you have currently memorized, feel free to call it good enough.

When your review is done, let's get into today's verse.

Say the following verse out loud 10 times:

“As he came near to the den where Daniel was, he cried out in a tone of anguish. The king declared to Daniel, ‘O Daniel, servant of the living God, has your God, whom you serve continually, been able to deliver you from the lions?’” (Daniel 6:20).

When you are done, recite the verse 10 times in a row from memory, doing your best not to look at the verse.

Great job! You got your next verse down!

You know the drill, throughout your day when you’re driving to work, taking a break from work, or cooking a meal, go over what you’ve memorized so far to keep reinforcing it in your mind.

Tomorrow you’ll quickly review what you learned today and add another verse to it.

If you don’t feel confident you’ve truly memorized today’s verse, consider listening through the chapter again.

See you tomorrow!

God bless.

Daniel 6:21

Today you are going to memorize Daniel 6:21.

After you review what you have already learned, you are going to memorize today's verse using the 10-10-10 Method.

Let's begin.

Let's review the verse you learned yesterday by reciting it 10 times from memory. Glance over it if you need a refresher.

"As he came near to the den where Daniel was, he cried out in a tone of anguish. The king declared to Daniel, 'O Daniel, servant of the living God, has your God, whom you serve continually, been able to deliver you from the lions?'" (Daniel 6:20).

Now you're going to review all the verses you have memorized up to this point by reciting them 10 times. You can find it in the prep work chapter for this week if you need a refresher. If after three times you feel confident in your ability to recite all the verses you have currently memorized, feel free to call it good enough.

When your review is done, let's get into today's verse.

Say the following verse out loud 10 times:

"Then Daniel said to the king, 'O king, live forever!'" (Daniel 6:21).

When you are done, recite the verse 10 times in a row from memory, doing your best not to look at the verse.

Great job! You got your next verse down!

You know the drill, throughout your day when you're driving to work, taking a break from work, or cooking a meal, go over what you've memorized so far to keep reinforcing it in your mind.

Tomorrow you'll quickly review what you learned today and add another verse to it.

If you don't feel confident you've truly memorized today's verse, consider listening through the chapter again.

See you tomorrow!

God bless.

Daniel 6:22

Today you are going to memorize Daniel 6:22.

After you review what you have already learned, you are going to memorize today's verse using the 10-10-10 Method.

Let's begin.

Let's review the verse you learned yesterday by reciting it 10 times from memory. Glance over it if you need a refresher.

"Then Daniel said to the king, 'O king, live forever!'" (Daniel 6:21).

Now you're going to review all the verses you have memorized up to this point by reciting them 10 times. You can find it in the prep work chapter for this week if you need a refresher. If after three times you feel confident in your ability to recite all the verses you have currently memorized, feel free to call it good enough.

When your review is done, let's get into today's verse.

Say the following verse out loud 10 times:

"'My God sent his angel and shut the lions' mouths, and they have not

harmed me, because I was found blameless before him; and also before you, O king, I have done no harm'" (Daniel 6:22).

When you are done, recite the verse 10 times in a row from memory, doing your best not to look at the verse.

Great job! You got your next verse down!

You know the drill, throughout your day when you're driving to work, taking a break from work, or cooking a meal, go over what you've memorized so far to keep reinforcing it in your mind.

Tomorrow you'll quickly review what you learned today and add another verse to it.

If you don't feel confident you've truly memorized today's verse, consider listening through the chapter again.

See you tomorrow!

God bless.

Daniel 6:23

Today you are going to memorize Daniel 6:23.

After you review what you have already learned, you are going to memorize today's verse using the 10-10-10 Method.

Let's begin.

Let's review the verse you learned yesterday by reciting it 10 times from memory. Glance over it if you need a refresher.

"'My God sent his angel and shut the lions' mouths, and they have not harmed me, because I was found blameless before him; and also before you, O king, I have done no harm'" (Daniel 6:22).

Now you're going to review all the verses you have memorized up to this point by reciting them 10 times. You can find it in the prep work chapter for this week if you need a refresher. If after three times you feel confident in your ability to recite all the verses you have currently memorized, feel free to call it good enough.

When your review is done, let's get into today's verse.

Say the following verse out loud 10 times:

"Then the king was exceedingly glad, and commanded that Daniel be taken up out of the den. So Daniel was taken up out of the den, and no kind of harm was found on him, because he had trusted in his God" (Daniel 6:23).

When you are done, recite the verse 10 times in a row from memory, doing your best not to look at the verse.

Great job! You got your next verse down!

You know the drill, throughout your day when you're driving to work, taking a break from work, or cooking a meal, go over what you've memorized so far to keep reinforcing it in your mind.

Tomorrow you'll quickly review what you learned today and add another verse to it.

If you don't feel confident you've truly memorized today's verse, consider listening through the chapter again.

See you tomorrow!

God bless.

Daniel 6:24

Today you are going to memorize Daniel 6:24.

After you review what you have already learned, you are going to memorize today's verse using the 10-10-10 Method.

Let's begin.

Let's review the verse you learned yesterday by reciting it 10 times from memory. Glance over it if you need a refresher.

"Then the king was exceedingly glad, and commanded that Daniel be taken up out of the den. So Daniel was taken up out of the den, and no kind of harm was found on him, because he had trusted in his God" (Daniel 6:23).

Now you're going to review all the verses you have memorized up to this point by reciting them 10 times. You can find it in the prep work chapter for this week if you need a refresher. If after three times you feel confident in your ability to recite all the verses you have currently memorized, feel free to call it good enough.

When your review is done, let's get into today's verse.

Say the following verse out loud 10 times:

"And the king commanded, and those men who had maliciously accused Daniel were brought and cast into the den of lions—they, their children, and their wives. And before they reached the bottom of the den, the lions overpowered them and broke all their bones in pieces" (Daniel 6:24).

When you are done, recite the verse 10 times in a row from memory, doing your best not to look at the verse.

Great job! You got your next verse down!

You know the drill, throughout your day when you're driving to work, taking a break from work, or cooking a meal, go over what you've memorized so far to keep reinforcing it in your mind.

Tomorrow you have the optional prep work for the last block of 4 verses. Though it's not mandatory, I can't stress enough how beneficial it will be moving forward.

If you plan to skip it, simply move to the following chapter to begin memorizing the first verse of the last block of 4 verses.

If you don't feel confident you've truly memorized today's verse, consider listening through the chapter again.

See you tomorrow!

God bless.

Week 5 Prep Work

If you are here, that tells me you are ready for your last block of verses to memorize.

Great job so far. I know it takes a lot of time and effort to memorize scripture and I hope all that time and effort has been a joyful experience.

Just like with the first round of prep work, this is completely optional.

You are not required to do this to memorize the last block of 4 verses.

But like I said before, it will make the task much easier.

If you are not up for the prep work, feel free to skip this chapter.

If you are willing to give it a shot, get ready to read the last 4 verses out loud 50 times which will take you about 40 minutes.

If you don't have 40 minutes, run through them 25 times which will only take you about 20 minutes.

Or commit to whatever you can.

Anything and everything you do here will help moving forward.

Please note, I left the verse numbers in the passage for your reference only.

When you are ready, begin.

25 Then King Darius wrote to all the peoples, nations, and languages that dwell in all the earth: "Peace be multiplied to you. 26 I make a decree, that in all my royal dominion people are to tremble and fear before the God of Daniel, for he is the living God, enduring forever; his kingdom shall never be destroyed, and his dominion shall be to the end. 27 He delivers and rescues; he works signs and wonders in heaven and on earth, he who has saved Daniel from the power of the lions." 28 So this Daniel prospered during the reign of Darius and the reign of Cyrus the Persian. (Daniel 6:25-28)

See you tomorrow!

Daniel 6:25

Today you are going to memorize Daniel 6:25.

After you review what you have already learned, you are going to memorize today's verse using the 10-10-10 Method.

Let's begin.

Let's review the verse you learned last by reciting it 10 times from memory. Glance over it if you need a refresher.

"And the king commanded, and those men who had maliciously accused Daniel were brought and cast into the den of lions—they, their children, and their wives. And before they reached the bottom of the den, the lions overpowered them and broke all their bones in pieces" (Daniel 6:24).

Now you're going to review all the verses you have memorized up to this point by reciting them 10 times. You can find it in the prep work chapter for this week if you need a refresher. If after three times you feel confident in your ability to recite all the verses you have currently memorized, feel free to call it good enough.

When your review is done, let's get into today's verse.

Say the following verse out loud 10 times:

"Then King Darius wrote to all the peoples, nations, and languages that dwell in all the earth: 'Peace be multiplied to you'" (Daniel 6:25).

When you are done, recite the verse 10 times in a row from memory, doing your best not to look at the verse.

Great job! You got your next verse down!

You know the drill, throughout your day when you're driving to work, taking a break from work, or cooking a meal, go over what you've memorized so far to keep reinforcing it in your mind.

Tomorrow you'll quickly review what you learned today and add another verse to it.

If you don't feel confident you've truly memorized today's verse, consider listening through the chapter again.

See you tomorrow!

God bless.

Daniel 6:26

Today you are going to memorize Daniel 6:26.

After you review what you have already learned, you are going to memorize today's verse using the 10-10-10 Method.

Let's begin.

Let's review the verse you learned last by reciting it 10 times from memory. Glance over it if you need a refresher.

"Then King Darius wrote to all the peoples, nations, and languages that dwell in all the earth: 'Peace be multiplied to you'" (Daniel 6:25).

Now you're going to review all the verses you have memorized up to this point by reciting them 10 times. You can find it in the prep work chapter for this week if you need a refresher. If after three times you feel confident in your ability to recite all the verses you have currently memorized, feel free to call it good enough.

When your review is done, let's get into today's verse.

Say the following verse out loud 10 times:

"'I make a decree, that in all my royal dominion people are to tremble and fear before the God of Daniel, for he is the living God, enduring forever; his kingdom shall never be destroyed, and his dominion shall be to the end'" (Daniel 6:26).

When you are done, recite the verse 10 times in a row from memory, doing your best not to look at the verse.

Great job! You got your next verse down!

You know the drill, throughout your day when you're driving to work, taking a break from work, or cooking a meal, go over what you've memorized so far to keep reinforcing it in your mind.

Tomorrow you'll quickly review what you learned today and add another verse to it.

If you don't feel confident you've truly memorized today's verse, consider listening through the chapter again.

See you tomorrow!

God bless.

Daniel 6:27

Today you are going to memorize Daniel 6:27.

After you review what you have already learned, you are going to memorize today's verse using the 10-10-10 Method.

Let's begin.

Let's review the verse you learned last by reciting it 10 times from memory. Glance over it if you need a refresher.

"'I make a decree, that in all my royal dominion people are to tremble and fear before the God of Daniel, for he is the living God, enduring forever; his kingdom shall never be destroyed, and his dominion shall be to the end'" (Daniel 6:26).

Now you're going to review all the verses you have memorized up to this point by reciting them 10 times. You can find it in the prep work chapter for this week if you need a refresher. If after three times you feel confident in your ability to recite all the verses you have currently memorized, feel free to call it good enough.

When your review is done, let's get into today's verse.

Say the following verse out loud 10 times:

"'He delivers and rescues; he works signs and wonders in heaven and on earth, he who has saved Daniel from the power of the lions'" (Daniel 6:27).

When you are done, recite the verse 10 times in a row from memory, doing your best not to look at the verse.

Great job! You got your next verse down!

You know the drill, throughout your day when you're driving to work, taking a break from work, or cooking a meal, go over what you've memorized so far to keep reinforcing it in your mind.

Tomorrow you'll quickly review what you learned today and add another verse to it.

If you don't feel confident you've truly memorized today's verse, consider listening through the chapter again.

See you tomorrow!

God bless.

Daniel 6:28

Today you are going to memorize Daniel 6:28.

After you review what you have already learned, you are going to memorize today's verse using the 10-10-10 Method.

Let's begin.

Let's review the verse you learned yesterday by reciting it 10 times from memory. Glance over it if you need a refresher.

"'He delivers and rescues; he works signs and wonders in heaven and on earth, he who has saved Daniel from the power of the lions'" (Daniel 6:27).

Now you're going to review all the verses you have memorized up to this point by reciting them 10 times. You can find it in the prep work chapter for this week if you need a refresher. If after three times you feel confident in your ability to recite all the verses you have currently memorized, feel free to call it good enough.

When your review is done, let's get into today's verse.

Say the following verse out loud 10 times:

"So this Daniel prospered during the reign of Darius and the reign of Cyrus the Persian" (Daniel 6:28).

When you are done, recite the verse 10 times in a row from memory, doing your best not to look at the verse.

Great job! You got your last verse down!

You know the drill, throughout your day when you're driving to work, taking a break from work, or cooking a meal, go over what you've memorized so far to keep reinforcing it in your mind.

If you don't feel confident you've truly memorized today's verse, consider listening through the chapter again.

God bless.

Conclusion

If you are here, I hope that means you have fully memorized Daniel 6.

I hope the experience was rewarding and enriching as you sealed part of God's Word in your heart.

I recommend reciting the full passage every day for the next 30 days to truly solidify that piece of scripture in your mind.

Once you're done, consider memorizing another passage or even an entire book of the Bible!

Lastly, if you have enjoyed this book, do consider leaving a review. I look forward to seeing your feedback.

May God bless you on your journey to further know Him, and I leave you with these two verses, "All Scripture is breathed out by God and profitable for teaching, for reproof, for correction, and for training in righteousness, that the man of God may be complete, equipped for every good work" (2 Timothy 3:16-17).

www.ingramcontent.com/pod-product-compliance
Lightning Source LLC
Chambersburg PA
CBHW030349100526
44592CB00010B/885
* 9 7 8 1 9 5 2 3 8 1 6 3 8 *